STEP BY STEP

STEP BY STEP

The Path to Self-Improvement through Kaizen

LOUISE IVORY

Advise the Heart

Contents

First Printing, 2024

ISBN: 979-8-8692-5917-2
EISBN: 979-8-8692-5918-9

I

Introduction

How do you embark on the journey of transforming your life? Is it something that happens overnight? The answer, without a doubt, is a firm "no!" Changing even the smallest aspect of your life requires patience, commitment, and effort. We, as human beings, are creatures of habit, and those habits become deeply rooted in our psyche over time. This is a physical phenomenon that can be observed in the brain, and we'll delve deeper into this concept later in this book.

Despite our intuitive understanding of this

process, many of us still believe that we can make drastic changes to our lives on a whim. If you've ever promised yourself that you'll start a new training program tomorrow, involving rigorous gym sessions four times a week and cutting your caloric intake in half, then you're not alone in feeling overwhelmed.

Fortunately, there's a better approach: Kaizen. This term originates from Japanese and Chinese languages, meaning "improvement." It represents a methodical approach to self-improvement, where small, incremental changes lead to significant progress over time. Remember the old adage: every long journey begins with a single step. And what is a thousand-mile journey but a series of single steps?

When we view challenges through this lens, they become more manageable and achievable. In this book, you'll discover how to harness the power of Kaizen and apply it to every aspect of your life, whether it's enhancing your relationships, improving your fitness, optimizing your health, growing your business, or any other area you wish to develop.

Get ready to transform your life for the better, one step at a time.

Why We Need Kaizen

Before we dive into the intricacies of what Kaizen entails and why it's effective, let's first explore the alternative approach and understand its significance.

As mentioned briefly earlier, many of us tend to impulsively pursue self-improvement by attempting to change everything all at once. For instance, starting a new training program that involves intense workouts four times a week and drastically reducing calorie intake is a scenario that resonates with many. Perhaps you've found yourself in a similar situation?

The challenge with this approach is that it overlooks key aspects of human psychology and the realities of our daily lives. Consider this: if you're currently not in the best shape, it's likely because you're not exercising enough and not eating properly. But why is that the case? It's often because you're exhausted and lacking motivation to engage in these activities. After a long day, coming home feeling drained, it's understandable that the idea of intense workouts seems daunting.

Expecting yourself to suddenly summon the energy for such a demanding routine is unrealistic. Going from feeling too tired to exercise at all to committing to four workouts a week is a significant leap. Let's break down what that entails: changing into gym clothes after work, driving to the gym, showering afterward, and then commuting back home. This can easily consume two hours, effectively adding a full working day to your schedule. Can you see the challenge here?

Moreover, this approach requires you to adapt to numerous new habits simultaneously while unlearning old ones. And if that's not enough, now you're also planning to consume significantly fewer calories while exerting twice the effort. It's a daunting prospect, to say the least.

Neuroscience plays a crucial role in this process. Our brains are remarkably adaptable, capable of restructuring themselves based on our behaviors. While this adaptability is beneficial for forming new habits, it can also work against us when attempting drastic changes. The brain establishes strong connections between repeated actions, making it challenging to break established patterns.

Attempting wholesale changes across multiple habits simultaneously is often futile. This is where Kaizen shines. It offers a powerful and transformative approach by focusing on gradual, sustainable improvements. In the next chapter, we'll delve deeper into Kaizen and how to leverage its effectiveness to the fullest.

How it Happens

You might be wondering how we still find ourselves drawn to the idea of making massive changes to our lives overnight, despite understanding the challenges involved. There are a few reasons for this.

Firstly, the allure of quick and dramatic transformations is undeniable. The idea that everything can change in a single day is incredibly enticing. It's natural for us to be captivated by this notion.

Secondly, the media plays a significant role in shaping our perceptions. Advertising agencies often promote a one-and-done approach to self-transformation because it aligns with their goals. Gyms, for instance, encourage us to buy expensive memberships, workout equipment, and supplements, leading us to believe that these purchases will magically solve our fitness challenges. However, the reality is often different, leaving us feeling guilty about spending money without seeing desired results.

It's essential to recognize these influences and

understand that lasting change requires a more gradual and sustainable approach. Kaizen provides the framework to make consistent progress over time, focusing on small improvements that add up to significant transformations. In the following chapters, we'll delve deeper into the principles of Kaizen and how to apply them effectively to achieve your goals.

3

Kaizen in its Original Context: Business

Kaizen is a term embraced by many in the self-improvement community, resonating with those striving for greater happiness, fitness, wealth, and wisdom. Originating as a business concept, understanding its roots in this context can enhance our comprehension and application of it in our lives. If you're involved in business, you'll find these insights valuable for their inherent benefits.

The Origin of Kaizen

The word "kaizen" translates to "improvement" or "change for the better" in Japanese, specifically emphasizing continuous improvement through small changes. Initially adopted in the business realm, particularly within methodologies like Toyota's, Kaizen has proven effective in enhancing processes and later extended into self-improvement practices. While self-help literature often simplifies Kaizen or misinterprets its core principles, understanding its strict business interpretation provides a solid foundation for its application.

Types of Kaizen

In its original business context, Kaizen is categorized into flow kaizen and process kaizen. Flow kaizen examines entire workflows, seeking opportunities for improvement across various stages. Conversely, process kaizen focuses on refining individual processes to their optimal state.

Kaizen operates from a "bottom-up" approach, emphasizing small changes at fundamental levels that yield significant improvements. This methodology isn't limited to business; it can be applied to personal routines effectively.

Simplify and Eliminate Waste

Furthermore, Kaizen involves identifying and eliminating waste within processes. This waste could be errors, excess processing, overproduction, waiting times, inventory issues, inefficient transportation, unnecessary movement, or underutilized talents. While these concepts may seem business-centric, they hold immense potential when applied to personal routines and workflows.

For instance, consider optimizing your writing process for a blog. By streamlining steps and eliminating redundant tasks, you can save time and increase productivity significantly. Kaizen encourages constant evaluation and refinement to uncover opportunities for improvement in all aspects of life.

Personal Application of Kaizen

While Kaizen principles are often associated

with business environments, they can be incredibly powerful when applied to personal life. Let's explore how you can leverage Kaizen to enhance your daily routines and achieve your goals more effectively.

Imagine applying Kaizen to your morning routine. Instead of trying to overhaul your entire morning in one go, focus on making small, manageable changes. For example, start by waking up five minutes earlier each day to incorporate a brief meditation or stretching session. Over time, gradually increase the duration or intensity of these activities.

Similarly, in your work or study habits, identify areas where small improvements can lead to significant outcomes. Perhaps you can allocate specific time blocks for focused work without distractions, or implement a system to organize tasks more efficiently.

Kaizen encourages a mindset of continuous improvement, where every small step forward contributes to larger progress. By breaking down your goals into manageable tasks and consistently making incremental improvements, you'll experience noticeable growth and achievements over time.

Examples of Personal Kaizen Practices

Here are some examples of how Kaizen can be applied to personal life:

1. **Health and Fitness:** Instead of aiming for drastic changes in diet or exercise routines, focus on making small adjustments such as adding more vegetables to your meals or taking short walks during breaks.

2. **Time Management:** Implement time-blocking techniques to allocate dedicated periods for different tasks, allowing you to work more efficiently and avoid multitasking.

3. **Learning and Skill Development:** Dedicate a few minutes each day to practice a new skill or review course material, gradually building mastery over time.

4. **Relationships:** Incorporate daily rituals such as expressing gratitude or actively listening

to loved ones, strengthening bonds and fostering positive interactions.

Remember, the key to successful Kaizen is consistency and patience. Celebrate each small improvement along the way and trust in the cumulative impact of these continuous efforts.

Financial Management:

Take a Kaizen approach to your finances by setting small, achievable savings goals each week or month. Look for areas where you can reduce unnecessary spending, such as dining out less frequently or finding more cost-effective alternatives for everyday expenses. Over time, these small changes can lead to significant savings and financial stability.

Mindfulness and Well-being:

Incorporate Kaizen into your mindfulness practices by starting with just a few minutes of meditation or deep breathing exercises each day. Gradually increase the duration or explore different techniques to find what works best for you. Similarly, prioritize self-care activities such as getting adequate sleep, staying hydrated, and engaging in activities that bring you joy and relaxation.

Personal Development:

Apply Kaizen principles to your personal growth journey by setting achievable goals for learning and development. Whether it's reading a few pages of a book each day, attending workshops or courses, or practicing a new skill regularly, consistent effort over time can lead to substantial progress and mastery.

Emotional Intelligence:

Work on enhancing your emotional intelligence through small, mindful practices such as practicing empathy, active listening, and managing stress effectively. Take time to reflect on your emotions and responses in various situations, and look for opportunities to improve your emotional awareness and resilience gradually.

Environmental Impact:

Contribute to a sustainable future by adopting Kaizen practices in reducing waste and conserving resources. Start by making small changes in your daily habits, such as recycling more, using reusable products, conserving energy and water, and supporting eco-friendly initiatives in your community.

Social Connections:

Nurture your relationships by practicing Kaizen in your interactions with others. Make small gestures of kindness, such as sending a thoughtful message, expressing appreciation, or actively engaging in meaningful conversations. These small acts can strengthen bonds and create a positive impact on your social connections.

Conclusion:

Kaizen is a powerful philosophy that empowers continuous improvement and growth in every aspect of life. By embracing small, incremental changes and maintaining a mindset of progress, you can transform challenges into opportunities for learning and development. Remember, every step forward, no matter how small, brings you closer to your goals and aspirations.

4

Kaizen Concepts to Consider

Kaizen becomes even more impactful when we delve into the realm of additional business concepts like force multipliers and automation. These concepts aren't just limited to business; they can also revolutionize our personal lives.

Force Multipliers:

A force multiplier is essentially a tool or method that helps you achieve more in less time or with less effort. For instance, think of a hammer that allows you to nail more efficiently than using your bare hands. In business, force multipliers can range from advanced software running on computers to equipment like forklift trucks, significantly boosting productivity and output. However, it's crucial to use them wisely to avoid potential errors. This is where Kaizen comes in, ensuring that your systems are efficient and scalable, leading to sustainable growth.

Automation:

Automation involves streamlining business processes by using software or tools to perform tasks with minimal human intervention. It's a logical progression from force multiplication but comes with its own set of risks, such as potential errors if not monitored carefully. Smart business individuals constantly look for ways to automate tasks, freeing up time and resources for strategic planning and innovation. Additionally, automation can transform services into products, enhancing efficiency and scalability.

The 5S of Kaizen:

In business, the 5 'S' words associated with Kaizen are crucial for effective implementation:

- Seiri/Sorting: Keeping work areas organized and clutter-free.
- Seiton/Systematic Arrangement: Arranging items for efficient retrieval and logistics.
- Seiso/Shining: Maintaining cleanliness to reduce errors.
- Seiketsu/Standardizing: Using standardized processes for consistency and improvement.
- Shitsuke/Sustaining: Ensuring adherence to the previous four 'S' principles.

Kaikaku:

While Kaizen is powerful for gradual improvement, there are instances where drastic change is necessary, known as Kaikaku. This involves completely overhauling processes that are beyond repair, despite initial resistance. Knowing when to implement Kaikaku versus Kaizen is essential for successful business strategies.

Strategic Implementation of Force Multipliers:

When integrating force multipliers into your business or personal life, it's essential to strategize effectively. Identify areas where these tools can make a significant impact, such as automating repetitive tasks or using technology to enhance efficiency. For instance, in business, investing in advanced software can streamline customer service processes, leading to faster response times and improved customer satisfaction. Similarly, in personal life, using productivity apps or tools can help you manage tasks more effectively, freeing up time for other priorities.

Automation for Efficiency and Growth:

Automation plays a pivotal role in driving efficiency and fostering growth. Businesses can automate tasks like data entry, invoicing, and inventory management to reduce manual errors and save time. In the personal sphere, automation tools can simplify daily routines, such as setting reminders for important tasks, managing finances, or scheduling appointments. By leveraging automation intelligently, you can enhance productivity and focus on higher-value activities.

Applying the 5S Principles in Everyday Life:

The 5S principles of Kaizen—sorting, systematic arrangement, shining, standardizing, and sustaining—can be adapted to various aspects of daily life. For example, organizing your workspace at home or implementing a decluttering routine aligns with the sorting and systematic arrangement principles. Regular cleaning and maintenance contribute to the shining aspect, reducing distractions and promoting a conducive environment for productivity. Standardizing processes, such as meal planning or exercise routines, ensures consistency and efficiency. Lastly, sustaining these practices over time ensures continued improvement and a harmonious lifestyle.

Navigating Kaikaku:

Kaikaku, or drastic change, requires careful consideration and strategic planning. It's essential to assess whether incremental improvements (Kaizen) can address issues or if a fundamental transformation is necessary. In business, Kaikaku may involve reimagining business models, adopting disruptive technologies, or entering new markets. On a personal level, it could mean making bold career changes, reevaluating life goals, or pursuing new passions. Embracing Kaikaku when warranted can lead to breakthroughs and transformative experiences.

Balancing Innovation and Stability:

Striking a balance between innovation and stability is key to sustainable growth. While innovation drives progress and competitiveness, stability ensures continuity and reliability. Businesses must foster a culture of continuous improvement (Kaizen) while also embracing innovation (Kaikaku) to adapt to evolving market dynamics. Likewise, individuals can pursue personal growth by embracing change while maintaining stability in core values and responsibilities.

5

Kaizen for Getting Into Shape – Health and Fitness

Let's delve deeper into the practical application of Kaizen in our daily lives, starting with fitness.

Microworkouts for Health:

Microworkouts offer a refreshing approach to fitness by emphasizing small, consistent efforts every day. Instead of overwhelming yourself with intense gym sessions, consider incorporating brief exercises into your routine. For example, doing

20 press-ups in the morning or opting for stairs instead of the elevator can make a significant difference over time. These micro-exercises not only boost your metabolism but also lay the foundation for lasting habits.

Understanding Habit Formation:

The process of habit formation is fascinating yet often misunderstood. Contrary to the popular notion that it takes 30 days to form a habit, research suggests it's closer to 66 days on average. This means that consistent practice over roughly two months solidifies habits. Therefore, starting with manageable exercises and gradually increasing intensity is far more effective than attempting drastic changes right away. It's about building momentum and sustainability in your fitness journey.

True Kaizen for Fitness:

While microworkouts and calorie cuts are beneficial, true Kaizen in fitness involves taking a holistic approach. It's about examining every aspect of your lifestyle to identify what's hindering your fitness goals. This could mean looking beyond exercise and diet to factors like stress management, sleep quality, and overall well-being. By addressing these underlying elements, you create a more conducive environment for long-term health.

Efficiency in Fitness:

Efficiency plays a crucial role in maintaining a consistent fitness routine. Instead of adding more tasks to an already hectic schedule, focus on optimizing your existing activities. Evaluate which activities you can trim or modify to free up time and energy for fitness. For instance, reducing non-essential commitments or incorporating active breaks during work hours can create significant opportunities for exercise without overwhelming yourself.

Finding the Right Routine:

Finding the right workout routine involves aligning your exercise schedule with your natural rhythms and preferences. Whether it's early mornings for a refreshing start, lunch breaks for a midday boost, or post-work sessions to unwind, choose a time that works best for you. By syncing your exercise routine with your daily routine, you maximize efficiency and minimize disruptions, making it easier to stay consistent.

Incremental Improvements:

Small changes can lead to significant fitness improvements over time. Consider increasing daily movement by incorporating activities like walking, stretching, or using standing desks. These small tweaks not only burn extra calories but also encourage your body to adapt to an active lifestyle gradually. By focusing on incremental improvements, you build resilience and long-lasting fitness habits.

Lifestyle Optimization for Health:

Achieving optimal health isn't just about workouts; it's about optimizing your entire lifestyle. Identify areas where you can reclaim time, energy, and vitality. This could involve streamlining daily tasks, reducing stress through mindfulness practices, prioritizing quality sleep, and nurturing supportive relationships. By creating a holistic approach to wellness, you set yourself up for sustainable health and well-being.

In essence, embracing Kaizen in fitness is about making consistent, incremental changes that align with your goals and values. It's a journey of self-discovery, resilience, and lifelong health.

6

Kaizen for Personal Finance

Let's delve deeper into how the Kaizen approach can transform your personal finances, leading to wealth and security. Contrary to popular belief, it's not just about randomly slashing expenses like your morning latte (although, let's admit, they seem to get quite the blame!).

Efficient Budgeting for Financial Wellness:

Crafting a budget isn't just about assigning arbitrary numbers; it's about creating a roadmap that aligns with your income and long-term financial goals. Instead of setting unrealistic limits, track your spending patterns to understand where adjustments can be made. For instance, consider buying more affordable groceries or dining out less frequently. It's not about depriving yourself but rather finding smart ways to allocate your resources.

Tracking and Adjusting:

Have you ever meticulously planned your budget only to see it crumble when unexpected expenses pop up? You're not alone; this is a common struggle for many. The key is to track your spending diligently and be ready to adjust your budget as needed. For example, if you overspend on groceries one week, find areas where you can cut back to balance it out. It's about being flexible and proactive in managing your finances.

Prepare for the Unexpected:

Life's surprises, like losing a card or needing to replace a costly item, can throw off even the best budgets. That's why it's essential to allocate a buffer amount in your budget to handle these unforeseen expenses. Over time, you'll learn to anticipate and plan for such occurrences, reducing their impact on your financial stability.

Automate Your Finances:

Automation can be a powerful ally in managing your money efficiently. Set up automatic transfers to separate accounts for different purposes, such as expenses, savings, and investments. This way, you stay within your budget effortlessly and avoid the temptation to overspend. Automating bill payments and savings contributions ensures you never miss a deadline and stay on track with your financial goals.

Reward Your Progress:

Celebrating your financial milestones is crucial to staying motivated and committed to your budgeting efforts. Consider rewarding yourself when you stick to your budget or achieve savings targets. This positive reinforcement not only feels great but also reinforces good financial habits. Whether it's treating yourself to a small indulgence or saving for a bigger goal, rewards keep you engaged in your financial journey.

Harness Technology:

In today's digital age, there's a wealth of financial tools and apps that can streamline budgeting and provide valuable insights. Apps like Emma categorize your spending, set realistic targets, and alert you when you're veering off budget. They act as your personal financial assistant, helping you make informed decisions and stay accountable to your financial plan.

The Kaizen Mindset:

At its core, Kaizen is about continuous improvement through small, manageable steps. Apply this mindset to your finances by making incremental changes that lead to significant progress over time. Whether it's optimizing your spending, reducing debt, or increasing savings, every small adjustment counts. By embracing the Kaizen approach, you create a sustainable financial framework that supports your long-term financial well-being.

In conclusion, Kaizen empowers you to take control of your finances, one step at a time. It's not about making drastic changes overnight but rather about making consistent, purposeful choices that align with your financial goals. Start small, stay consistent, and watch your financial health flourish over time.

7

❧

Kaizen for Productivity and Business

Transforming Your Finances with Kaizen: A Roadmap to Wealth

In the realm of personal finance, adopting a Kaizen approach can be a game-changer. It's not just about cutting expenses randomly or making drastic changes; it's about implementing small, strategic improvements that lead to long-term financial health and prosperity. Let's delve deeper into how the Kaizen philosophy can revolutionize your financial journey.

Setting the Stage with Efficient Budgeting:

The cornerstone of financial well-being is a well-crafted budget. However, creating a budget goes beyond assigning numbers to categories; it's about understanding your income, expenses, and financial goals. Start by accurately assessing your cash flow—how much money you have coming in and how much you're spending. This data-driven approach lays the foundation for smart financial decisions.

Tracking and Adjusting:

A common pitfall in budgeting is setting unrealistic limits without considering real-life spending patterns. This often leads to frustration and budget abandonment. Instead, adopt a proactive stance by tracking your expenses meticulously. Use tools like spreadsheets or budgeting apps to categorize expenditures and identify areas where adjustments can be made. For instance, if dining out frequently is straining your budget, explore cost-effective meal prep options to cut down on restaurant bills.

Prepare for the Unexpected:

Life is full of surprises, and financial planning should account for these unforeseen events. Build a buffer in your budget to handle emergencies or unexpected expenses. This buffer acts as a safety net, preventing minor setbacks from derailing your entire financial plan. Over time, as you track these unexpected costs, you'll gain insights into potential areas where you can further optimize your spending.

Automate Your Financial Systems:

One of the key principles of Kaizen is efficiency, and automation plays a pivotal role in achieving this efficiency in personal finance. Set up automatic transfers for savings, investments, and bill payments. Automation not only saves time but also eliminates the risk of forgetting important financial tasks. By streamlining your financial workflows, you free up mental bandwidth to focus on strategic money management.

Rewarding Financial Discipline:

Staying motivated on your financial journey is essential, and rewards can be powerful incentives. Consider incorporating rewards into your budgeting strategy. For instance, set savings milestones and treat yourself to a small indulgence when you reach them. This positive reinforcement reinforces good financial habits and keeps you inspired to stick to your budget.

Harnessing Technology for Financial Insights:

Technology has revolutionized personal finance management. Leverage budgeting apps and financial tools that provide real-time insights into your spending habits. These apps categorize transactions, track progress towards financial goals, and offer actionable recommendations. By harnessing the power of technology, you gain a holistic view of your finances and make informed decisions.

The Kaizen Mindset in Action:

At its core, Kaizen emphasizes continuous

improvement through small, incremental changes. Apply this mindset to your finances by identifying areas where minor adjustments can yield significant results. Whether it's negotiating better deals on recurring expenses, consolidating high-interest debt, or exploring investment opportunities, every small step contributes to your financial growth.

Building Financial Resilience:

Kaizen isn't just about optimizing spending; it's also about building resilience in the face of financial challenges. Consider diversifying your income streams, building an emergency fund, and investing in assets that generate passive income. These strategies create a robust financial foundation that can weather economic uncertainties and unexpected life events.

Educating and Empowering Yourself:

Lastly, invest in financial education and empower yourself with knowledge. Attend workshops, read books on personal finance, and seek guidance from financial advisors. The more informed you are, the better equipped you'll be to make sound financial decisions aligned with your goals and values.

In conclusion, adopting a Kaizen approach to personal finance is a journey of continuous improvement and empowerment. By focusing on small, manageable changes, leveraging technology, and staying disciplined, you pave the way for long-term financial success and fulfillment. Start today with a clear vision, strategic planning, and a commitment to financial well-being. Your financial future begins with each small, intentional step you take.

8

Life Hacks and Biohacks

Unlocking Your Potential with Life and Health Hacks

Embracing the Kaizen philosophy opens doors to transformative concepts like "life hacks" and "biohacks." These are small changes in lifestyle or health practices that can yield significant improvements in your overall well-being. However, amidst a sea of trendy hacks, it's crucial to discern the ones that genuinely work and integrate them into your daily life. When you feel better physically and mentally, you naturally perform better in all aspects of your life.

Optimizing Sleep Quality with Temperature:

Traditionally, we believed that ambient light played a central role in sleep quality. Yet, recent insights challenge this notion. Studies on indigenous communities reveal a fascinating pattern: their sleep rhythms are not solely dictated by light exposure but also by temperature fluctuations. Adjusting your sleeping environment by slightly opening a window can be a simple yet effective way to enhance sleep quality. Waking up refreshed sets a positive tone for the day ahead.

Mastering Morning Routines for Productivity:

Rising early has long been associated with productivity and success. However, it's not about sacrificing sleep but rather eliminating time wastage, especially the snooze button habit. Contrary to popular advice, a gentle hack involves briefly engaging with your phone upon waking. This small action, devoid of distractions like emails, triggers the production of cortisol, aiding in waking up naturally. Gradually, this routine primes you for a productive start each morning.

Enhancing Vitality with Thoughtful Supplementation:

While a balanced diet is ideal, supplements can bridge nutritional gaps and promote overall health. Natural supplements like Vitamin D, Omega 3, and Ashwagandha have shown to boost energy, cognitive function, and immune resilience. Incorporating these into your daily regimen can amplify your well-being, making other lifestyle changes easier and more effective. Additionally, consulting with a healthcare professional for personalized supplementation guidance ensures optimal health benefits.

Nurturing Inspiration and Focus:

Maintaining inspiration and focus is crucial for achieving goals. Engaging with enriching content like audiobooks during daily activities cultivates a focused mindset. Avoiding mindless distractions such as TV or aimless social media scrolling preserves mental clarity and fosters productivity. Furthermore, incorporating mindfulness practices like meditation or journaling can enhance creativity and problem-solving abilities.

Elevating Confidence and Productivity Through Attire:

Your clothing choices can significantly impact your mindset and interactions. Dressing in attire that reflects professionalism and productivity not only boosts self-confidence but also influences how others perceive and engage with you. Investing time in selecting appropriate attire is an investment in your overall effectiveness. Additionally, incorporating elements of personal style that resonate with your identity enhances comfort and confidence, contributing to a positive mindset throughout the day.

Exploring Intermittent Fasting for Health and Time Efficiency:

Intermittent fasting isn't just about weight management; it offers a host of potential health benefits, including increased energy and focus. By adopting intermittent fasting, you not only optimize your health but also reclaim time typically spent on breakfast preparation, contributing to a more efficient daily routine. However, it's essential to approach intermittent fasting mindfully, considering individual health needs and consulting with healthcare professionals as needed to ensure a safe and effective fasting protocol.

Incorporating these practical life and health hacks into your daily life aligns with the Kaizen philosophy of continuous improvement. Each small change contributes to your overall well-being, productivity, and success, creating a positive ripple effect in every aspect of your life. Embracing a holistic approach to self-care and growth empowers you to unlock your full potential and live a fulfilling life.

9

Finding Balance

Unlocking Your Potential with Life and Health Hacks

Embracing the Kaizen philosophy opens doors to transformative concepts like "life hacks" and "biohacks." These are small changes in lifestyle or health practices that can yield significant improvements in your overall well-being. However, amidst a sea of trendy hacks, it's crucial to discern the ones that genuinely work and integrate them into your daily life. When you feel better physically and mentally, you naturally perform better in all aspects of your life.

Optimizing Sleep Quality with Temperature:

Traditionally, we believed that ambient light played a central role in sleep quality. Yet, recent insights challenge this notion. Studies on indigenous communities reveal a fascinating pattern: their sleep rhythms are not solely dictated by light exposure but also by temperature fluctuations. Adjusting your sleeping environment by slightly opening a window can be a simple yet effective way to enhance sleep quality. Waking up refreshed sets a positive tone for the day ahead.

Mastering Morning Routines for Productivity:

Rising early has long been associated with productivity and success. However, it's not about sacrificing sleep but rather eliminating time wastage, especially the snooze button habit. Contrary to popular advice, a gentle hack involves briefly engaging with your phone upon waking. This small action, devoid of distractions like emails, triggers the production of cortisol, aiding in waking up naturally. Gradually, this routine primes you for a productive start each morning.

Enhancing Vitality with Thoughtful Supplementation:

While a balanced diet is ideal, supplements can bridge nutritional gaps and promote overall health. Natural supplements like Vitamin D, Omega 3, and Ashwagandha have shown to boost energy, cognitive function, and immune resilience. Incorporating these into your daily regimen can amplify your well-being, making other lifestyle changes easier and more effective. Additionally, consulting with a healthcare professional for personalized supplementation guidance ensures optimal health benefits.

Nurturing Inspiration and Focus:

Maintaining inspiration and focus is crucial for achieving goals. Engaging with enriching content like audiobooks during daily activities cultivates a focused mindset. Avoiding mindless distractions such as TV or aimless social media scrolling preserves mental clarity and fosters productivity. Furthermore, incorporating mindfulness practices like meditation or journaling can enhance creativity and problem-solving abilities.

Elevating Confidence and Productivity Through Attire:

Your clothing choices can significantly impact your mindset and interactions. Dressing in attire that reflects professionalism and productivity not only boosts self-confidence but also influences how others perceive and engage with you. Investing time in selecting appropriate attire is an investment in your overall effectiveness. Additionally, incorporating elements of personal style that resonate with your identity enhances comfort and confidence, contributing to a positive mindset throughout the day.

Exploring Intermittent Fasting for Health and Time Efficiency:

Intermittent fasting isn't just about weight management; it offers a host of potential health benefits, including increased energy and focus. By adopting intermittent fasting, you not only optimize your health but also reclaim time typically spent on breakfast preparation, contributing to a more efficient daily routine. However, it's essential to approach intermittent fasting mindfully, considering individual health needs and consulting with healthcare professionals as needed to ensure a safe and effective fasting protocol.

Incorporating these practical life and health hacks into your daily life aligns with the Kaizen philosophy of continuous improvement. Each small change contributes to your overall well-being, productivity, and success, creating a positive ripple effect in every aspect of your life. Embracing a holistic approach to self-care and growth empowers you to unlock your full potential and live a fulfilling life.

10

A Few Final Words

In summary, Kaizen is an exceptionally powerful tool that can make a significant difference in your life.

When applied effectively, it has the potential to revolutionize your life by guiding you to stop investing time and energy in trivial matters. You can enhance your budgeting skills, prioritize your health, work on your fitness goals, and boost your overall productivity.

However, it's crucial to also prioritize self-care

and relaxation. Remember to take breaks and unwind every now and then to maintain a healthy balance in your life.

As we wrap up our journey of self-discovery and empowerment, let's reflect on the profound impact of Kaizen. Here are the key insights to carry forward:

1. **Financial Empowerment:** Take charge of your finances by creating a budget aligned with your goals and regularly monitoring your spending patterns for smart adjustments.

2. **Holistic Health Biohacks:** Embrace small yet impactful changes like optimizing your sleep environment and cultivating positive morning habits for enhanced well-being.

3. **Nourish Your Body:** Consider integrating natural supplements such as Vitamin D, Omega 3, and Ashwagandha into your daily routine to support your energy levels, brain function, and emotional balance.

4. **Inspiration for Success:** Fuel your creativity and productivity by engaging in

activities that inspire you, like listening to motivational audiobooks or dressing confidently to boost your self-esteem.

5. **Mindful Nutrition:** Explore the benefits of intermittent fasting as a mindful approach to managing weight and promoting overall health.

As you continue on your personal growth journey, remember to prioritize self-care and allow yourself moments of rest and rejuvenation. Embrace the spirit of Kaizen as a gentle guide toward continuous improvement and fulfillment in every aspect of your life."